Get Out of Your

HEAD

and Into Your

HEART

A Journal for
Escaping the Spiral
of Toxic Thoughts
and Getting
Unstuck

THERESE WALSH

CASTLE POINT BOOKS

NEW YORK

www.castlepointbooks.com

The Castle Point Books trademark is owned by Castle Point Publishing, LLC.

Castle Point books are published and distributed by
St. Martin's Publishing Group.

ISBN 978-1-250- 27550-9 (trade paperback)

Our books may be purchased in bulk for promotional, educational, or business use. Please contact your local bookseller or the Macmillan Corporate and Premium Sales Department at 1-800-221-7945, extension 5442, or by email at MacmillanSpecialMarkets@macmillan.com.

First Edition: 2021

10 9 8 7 6 5 4 3 2 1

This journal belongs to:

....

FREE YOUR MIND &
unlock your potential!

You know that dark place you sometimes visit? The one where every version of yourself is awful, every decision is the wrong one, and every thought makes you feel even worse about yourself? That toxic spiral—what created it, what fuels it, why it persists, and how to break free of it—is what this book is all about. By honestly assessing that dark place, you'll come to better understand why it has persisted and drawn you in. Then you can begin to create an alternate space—a positive space—that will see you through the tough times to come and give you a whole new perspective on your hopes and dreams.

All you need to get unstuck is a willingness to do the hard work of excavating your truth, one small step at a time. If you're open to doing that, this guided journal can help you get out of your head and into your heart.

Stop a minute,
right where you are ...
TELL THAT IMPERIOUS
VOICE IN YOUR HEAD
TO BE STILL.

-BARBARA KINGSOLVER

Give Your Heart a Chance

The best way to approach reflection and internal work—like the work in this journal—is to begin with a calm and clear mind. Some people are able to meditate with ease, while others struggle to let go of their thoughts. Try this: Write down as many things as you can think of that bring you peace.

Whenever you feel your mind overriding your ability to focus on the exercises in this book, spend a minute or two reflecting on each of these peaceful thoughts with your eyes closed. Animate them in your mind and recall their place or promise in your life. Breathe.

Commit to the Work

It's one thing to say you want change in your life, and it's another to see it through. The secret sauce is your willingness and ability to work, and the thing that fuels that is your motivation. Why do you seek change? List as many reasons as you can.

Now tell each of those reasons that they're worth it.

Nothing will work UNLESS YOU DO.

-MAYA ANGELOU

The act of
STORYTELLING
is an act of
HEALING.

-CLEMANTINE WAMARIYA

Validate Yourself

Spend some time confirming your own life experience and any struggles you've endured. Share your stories with others if you can or write them here for yourself. What is the name of your burden? Use this space to tell it what you would say if you could speak with it directly.

What has this burden cost you?

Generate Power from the Dark

It can be empowering to document how you experience struggle. The next time you're in a cycle of negative thoughts, make a record here of what set it off, and how your thoughts spiral while in the moment. Do this every time you find yourself in a spiral. Add a checkmark beside those negative thoughts you find yourself revisiting.

Over time, you may see which negative thoughts hold the most power over you and even recognize a pattern—the path of your mind's spiral. You can use all of this to help prevent a spiral-in-progress.

Bookmark this page so you can easily find it when you feel a spiral coming on.

You can't study the
DARKNESS
by flooding it with
LIGHT.

EDWARD ABBEY

All people deserve your kindness, BUT NONE MORE SO THAN YOU.

-JUSTIN KAN

Make Yourself a Promise

As important as it is to document your mindset when in a downward spiral, it is just as important to avoid judging yourself or your potential when in a dark headspace. That's like going on a long road trip at night wearing sunglasses. The bad situation will be made worse. So don't do it. Instead, recognize the darkness when it comes and read the encouraging note you'll write to yourself below:

Stay Flexible

Sometimes obstacles stand in the way of our dreams, whether situational or within ourselves, and no amount of effort will make them vanish. In these instances, we might think about traveling to our goals in a different way, or even creating adjacent goals. Take the reins off your imagination and consider: What immovable component in your life stands in the way of your dreams, and how might you attain your goal in spite of that?

Fill in the following:

It might be harder for me to .... ,

but I could try ....

INTELLIGENCE
IS THE ABILITY TO
ADAPT TO CHANGE.

-STEPHEN HAWKING

MOST CYNICS ARE REALLY CRUSHED ROMANTICS:
they've been hurt,
they're sensitive,
and their cynicism is a shell
that's protecting this tiny,
dear part in them
that's still alive.

—JEFF BRIDGES

Call Out Your Cynicism

Sometimes we stunt our hopes and dreams without realizing it, due to a default skepticism we've acquired somewhere along the way. Take a moment to consider the doubts you hold about the achievability of your own dreams and write them here:

Can you see how your skepticism guards a deep sensitivity within?

Now look back at your negative spirals on page 8 and assess how many thoughts there are fueled by doubt. Circle those.

Unburden Yourself

Are you carrying secrets that make their way into your negative chatter?
Acknowledge them here, even if you need to write with your finger
instead of a pencil.

Now look back at your negative spirals on page 8 and assess how many
thoughts there are fueled by secrets. Imagine releasing those secrets.
How would you feel?

It is a truth
universally acknowledged
THAT SECRETS
ARE TOXIC.

-JANE RIDLEY

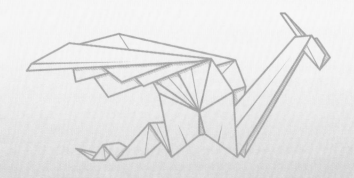

LET US BE OF CHEER,

remembering that
the misfortunes
hardest to bear

ARE THOSE WHICH
NEVER COME.

-AMY LOWELL

Name Your Paper Dragons

Often our worst enemy is our own imagination. Use this space to recall something you feared might happen, that would have been dreadful, but that did not happen. What false assumptions, if any, did you make?

Now look back at your negative spirals on page 8 and assess how many thoughts there are fueled by fear. How many of those fears are paper dragons, too, or are the result of imagining worst-case scenarios instead of most-likely scenarios? Extinguish those dragons by seeing them for what they are. Cross them off that page using a red pencil.

Debunk the Illogical

In recent days or months, when have you had irrational ideas, an all-or-nothing mentality, or an argument that falls apart when you revisit it on a better day? Record any illogical thoughts you've gotten stuck on below. Then write your best counterarguments against them.

THE HAPPINESS
OF YOUR LIFE

DEPENDS UPON
THE QUALITY OF
YOUR THOUGHTS.

–MARCUS AURELIUS

When you follow your heart,
you're never supposed to
do things because of what
you think people might say.

YOU DO IT FOR THE
OPPOSITE REASONS.

-WILL.I.AM

Refine Your Reasons

Think about how you're living your life right now. Are you following your agenda or someone else's? Ask yourself the following:

I want .... for myself because

....

....

I might be influenced by what ....

wants for me because ....

....

If it were up to me, I'd..

....

....

Express Yourself

What limitations have you placed on yourself or have others placed on you? When have you gotten stuck in a negative spiral thinking about those so-called limits? How could you push past those "walls" and express yourself with abandon?

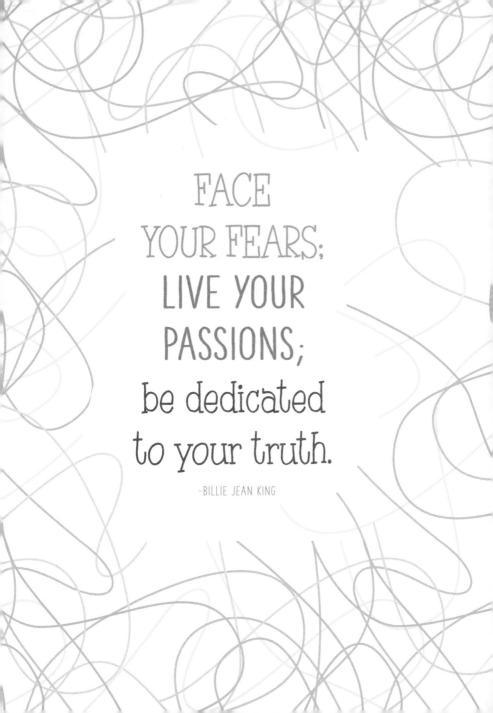

FACE
YOUR FEARS;
LIVE YOUR
PASSIONS;
be dedicated
to your truth.

−BILLIE JEAN KING

You're imperfect,
and you're wired
for struggle,

**BUT YOU ARE
WORTHY OF LOVE
AND BELONGING.**

-BRENÉ BROWN

Give the Boot to "Perfection"

Have you been asking too much of yourself in any area of your life, or even asking others to meet an unrealistic goal? Do you think that if only you were built differently, or thought differently, or had one or another ideal scenario, your life could be perfect? Consider how this might create a negative thought spiral that you don't deserve.

There is no such thing as perfect. Write your true qualities here, those that make you beautifully human:

Remember Yourself

Imagine who you could be without the baggage of your negative thoughts. What negative thoughts have weighed you down or made you different than you want to be? Use this space to take one of those thoughts and gently, kindly offer yourself guidance to cope with it.

What positive thoughts define your true inner spirit, strength, and resolve?

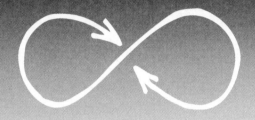

The paradox of trauma
is that it has both the
POWER TO DESTROY
and the power to
TRANSFORM
AND RESURRECT.

-PETER A. LEVINE

Out of the suffering have
emerged the strongest souls;

THE MOST MASSIVE
CHARACTERS ARE
SEARED WITH SCARS.

-KAHLIL GIBRAN

♡

Unearth the Roots

Consider your most pervasive negative thoughts. Do they trace back
to a particular time in your life, a lost dream, or even another person?
Pinpoint the root of each negative thought if you can, then write it here.
If you notice any commonalities or themes, make note of those.

Now ask yourself: What were the gifts of each
of those life experiences?

Know What Works

Think about the last time you were in a spiral, and what finally put an end to it. What self-talk or action or person provided you with the lifeline you needed? Maybe it's a walk, a coffee meet-up with a friend, or a good night of sleep. Make a list below:

The next time your go-to strategy for ending a downward spiral doesn't seem to be working, try one of these healthy actions.

You can make
bad choices and
find yourself in
a downward spiral
OR YOU CAN
FIND SOMETHING
THAT GETS YOU
OUT OF IT.

-RAY LAMONTAGNE

ALL THE
LITTLE THINGS
YOU NITPICK
IN YOUR HEAD,
NOBODY REALLY
CARES THAT MUCH
OUTSIDE YOUR HEAD.

-PENN BADGLEY

Release the Critic

Use this space to counter at least five nitpicky things you think about yourself. Spin your self-criticisms around to find a positive or humorous angle on the same subject. If you find it difficult, dig deeper and find the self-love you need.

1.

2.

3.

4.

5.

♡
Flip Your Regrets

It can be hard to see the gift in something painful. Acknowledging that lessons can come from hardships is an important step in overcoming the harm and pain. Consider some of your most profound regrets and ask yourself: What did each experience teach you about yourself, about someone else, about limits, about life? Write those here.

Is there a regret for which you can find no gift? Write that here, and then return to this page as you work through this book. You may unearth something after all.

I made decisions that
I regret, and I took them
as learning experiences...

I'M HUMAN,
NOT PERFECT,
LIKE ANYBODY ELSE.

QUEEN LATIFAH

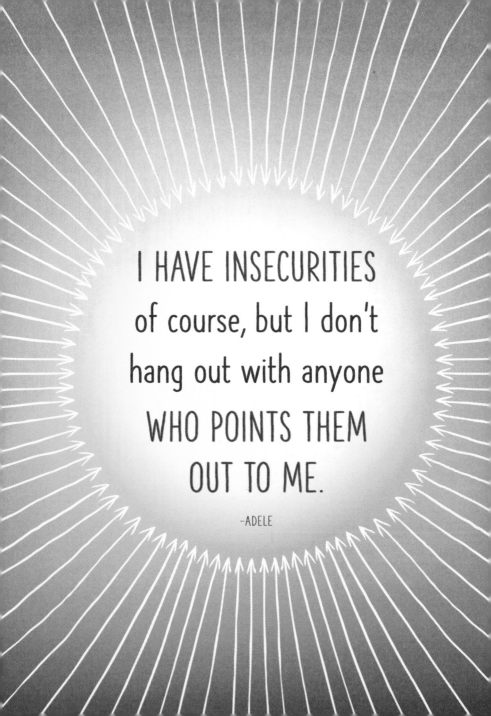

Manage Your Psychic Vampires

Not all of our negative thoughts originate from within. Who are the
people in your life that pull you off course and leave you depleted?
How can you limit or eliminate your exposure to them, especially
while focused on the hard work of trying to connect with yourself
at a deep level?

Alternatively, who would you like to spend more time with? Who leaves
you feeling energized and positive about yourself?

Take Stock

What "aha" moments have you experienced as you've progressed through this journal? These bright moments often lead to more of the same. Write them down and celebrate them here. How could you be gentler on yourself? How might you get out of your own head and enjoy life more? Where do you need to heal?

ALL WONDERS
YOU SEEK
ARE WITHIN
YOURSELF.

-SIR THOMAS BROWNE

Sometimes
the heart sees
WHAT IS INVISIBLE
TO THE EYE.

-H. JACKSON BROWN, JR.

Acknowledge Your Deepest Desires

Let your heart be heard today. List some of the things you want most in the world.

How are you working toward them? What aspects of your life support them?

What can you cut out of your life so that you have more time to live the life you want?

Challenge Your Negative Beliefs

Limiting beliefs can create a self-fulfilling prophecy if we're not careful. The first step in combating them is understanding what they are. What negative feelings about yourself seem most resistant to change?

Beside each of those beliefs, write at least one argument against it.

NEGATIVE THOUGHTS STICK AROUND BECAUSE WE BELIEVE THEM, not because we want them or choose them.

–ANDREW J. BERNSTEIN

All water has
a perfect memory
and is forever trying
TO GET BACK TO
WHERE IT WAS.

-TONI MORRISON

Resist the Old to Forge the New

We're all familiar with the saying "Old habits die hard." Long-held patterns can be difficult to break, even when they're habits of thought. But new patterns can be forged. Name a habit you've broken, or a new healthy habit you've created, and detail what it took for you to do that.

What self-talk did you use or what actions did you take to stay the course when you felt resistance?

Live This Moment

Chances are, your life and your brain are always busy. Interrupt that endless flow with inspired action. Look for ways to move forward today, even if your actions seem small to you in the moment. What can you do right now, today, even this very hour, to help yourself? How might you start to add more love and joy to your life?

EACH MOMENT
IS A PLACE
YOU'VE NEVER
BEEN.

–MARK STRAND

A man who has not passed

THROUGH
THE INFERNO
OF HIS
PASSIONS

has never overcome them.

-CARL JUNG

Remember Your Strength

You've gone through tough times before. You've been challenged. You've succeeded at things that you never would have thought possible. Recall those times of strength now, and those instances of perseverance and success. List as many as you can below.

Know you are capable of this journey because you've worn these shoes before, even if you've never before walked this path.

Practice Release

All of our unmet dreams lie in the future, yet so much of the time we spend energy on the past. What past mistakes made by yourself or others can you release right now? If not today, what will it take for you to free them?

I decided I can't pay a
person to rewind time,

SO I MAY
AS WELL
GET OVER IT.

SERENA WILLIAMS

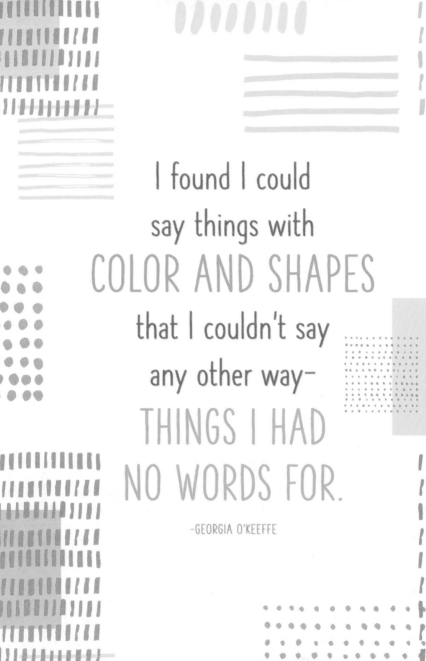

I found I could
say things with
COLOR AND SHAPES
that I couldn't say
any other way—
THINGS I HAD
NO WORDS FOR.

−GEORGIA O'KEEFFE

Express Yourself

Some people communicate their feelings through words, while others prefer visual art, music, or working with their hands. How do you best express yourself? If you don't express yourself that way on a regular basis, how can you make space in your life so that you can?

If any of the exercises in this book have been especially difficult for you to get your head around, consider musing over them while engaged in your favorite mode of self-expression.

Invent a Model Self

Imagine yourself a year from now, or ten. You've made choices that have put you in a good place. You are happy. How does Future You think about the challenges before you today? How might they nudge you toward your destiny?

Imagine for yourself
a character,
a model personality,
whose example you
determine to follow,
in private as well
as in public.

—EPICTETUS

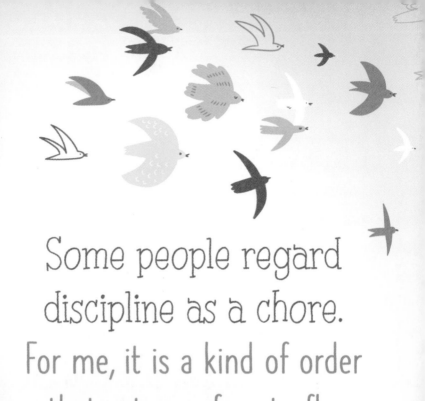

Some people regard discipline as a chore. For me, it is a kind of order that sets me free to fly.

-JULIE ANDREWS

Customize Your Tools

What habits feed your spirit and keep you in a healthy mindset? How much you thrive may depend upon how you sleep or eat, when you work, the level of solitude and/or sound with which you work, how you break up your day, the involvement of music or art, your level of organization, and so on. Take some time to experiment, then list below some of the things that help you be your most positive, forward-focused self every day.

If you aren't able to create your best conditions regularly, what small steps might you take to move closer to them in the future? What one thing can you do now to create better vibes for yourself?

Build on Your Toolbox

Every challenge that pushes you out of your head and into your heart may test you, but many will bring you new revelations about yourself— your skills, your tendencies, your potential, your ever-expanding dreams. Take time to document those revelations when you reach what feels like a milestone. How did you get there? What ability has evolved? What new workplace habit has emerged as a favorite? What new thing have you discovered that shuts down a negative cycle?

As you change, so will your knowledge about yourself. Add everything you see as an asset to your mental toolbox.

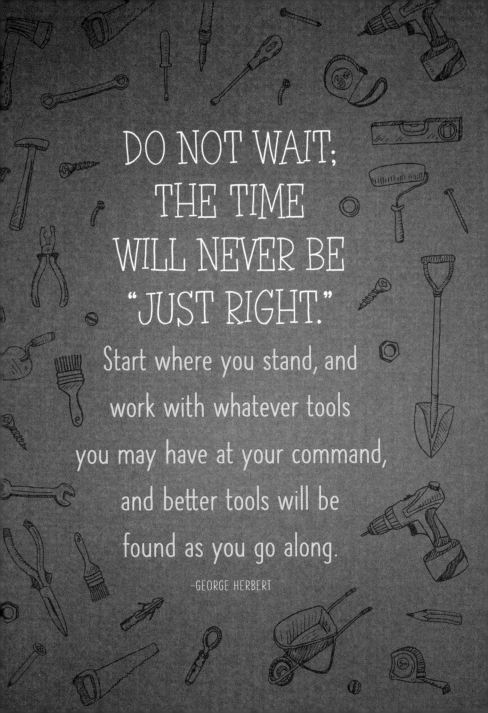

DO NOT WAIT;
THE TIME
WILL NEVER BE
"JUST RIGHT."

Start where you stand, and
work with whatever tools
you may have at your command,
and better tools will be
found as you go along.

-GEORGE HERBERT

THE CONSEQUENCES OF AN ACT

affect the probability of its occurring again.

–B. F. SKINNER

♡

Create a Catalytic Cycle

Imagine one of the bigger dreams you have for yourself. How many small goals must be reached in order for that dream goal to be attained? List as many of those goals as you can.

Reward yourself once you reach each of these small goals, and in this way build energy for each next step.

♡
Accept Uncertainty

Some people love risk, though many do not. But sometimes you have to risk in order to move forward in truth. How comfortable are you making risky decisions? What goals do you have that ask you to risk something? What is the worst thing that can happen if you fail? What is the best?

Complete the following:

I am willing to risk

for a chance to attain

THE TASK WE MUST SET FOR OURSELVES

is not to feel secure,
but to be able to

TOLERATE INSECURITY.

-ERICH FROMM

DON'T TAKE YOURSELF TOO SERIOUSLY.

Know when to laugh at yourself, and find a way to laugh at obstacles that inevitably present themselves.

−HALLE BERRY

Lighten Up

Consider a time when you failed to achieve a goal through a comedy of errors. Were you able to laugh at yourself? Can you laugh about it now? Retell the story below and look for the light side as you do.

♡

Metamorphose Yourself

We are all filled with unrealized potentials. We might have been virtuosos with the violin, if only we'd been handed the instrument at a young age. Life brings us the opportunities that it does, but other times we are able to make them for ourselves. Turn off your every impulse to the contrary, and spend this page letting loose your imagination. You are like a caterpillar who is about to turn into something new. What will you become? Describe your new self here:

There is nothing in a
caterpillar that tells you

IT'S GOING TO BE
A BUTTERFLY.

-R. BUCKMINSTER FULLER

Everything that slows us down and forces patience, everything that sets us back into the slow circles of nature, is a help.

GARDENING IS AN INSTRUMENT OF GRACE.

—MAY SARTON

Grow Mental Space

Some people are naturals at meditation, while others take more time to find their way into it. A long drive, a hot shower or bath, working clay or dough or the land—these can all help quiet a busy mind. Consider what helps you hear the less dominant but still important messages from your innermost self. What activities allow you time to connect with your center, to relax and think?

Is there an activity that used to ground you that you've lost touch with, and how might you reintroduce it?

Reach Beyond Your Own Experience

You're not the only one trying to get out of your own head and live your life more joyfully. Ask those you trust to share their experiences with you, if they're willing. Ask what they do to break a cycle of negative thoughts when they begin to spiral. Write down their stories or strategies here:

Try one or more of them the next time your own strategies don't work.

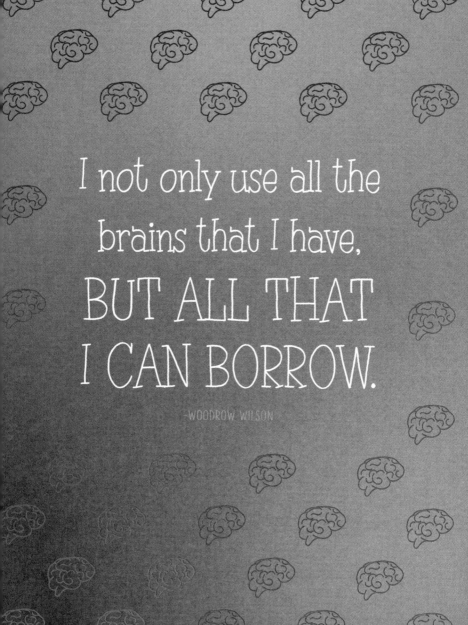

I not only use all the brains that I have, BUT ALL THAT I CAN BORROW.

-WOODROW WILSON

[IF] YOU ARE MAKING MISTAKES,
then you are making new things,
TRYING NEW THINGS, LEARNING,
living, pushing yourself,
CHANGING YOURSELF,
changing your world.

—NEIL GAIMAN

Learn the Value of Mistakes

Everything that you try can teach you something about yourself. Even the "bad stuff"—even the mistakes. Because all of that means you *are* moving forward. Even if you have to go back. Even if you have to go sideways. All of it is progress and knowledge and can help you find the way that will ultimately work.

Consider something you tried that did not succeed. How did you react?

How did those mistakes inspire your new direction or next steps?

Call Out—and Reject—Excuses

Be honest with yourself and write out every excuse you can think of
for not following your heart's desire: How many of those excuses exist
because change seems too difficult?

Beside them, write a single, small action you can take today that will put
you one step closer to reaching your ultimate goal.

OPPORTUNITY

is missed by most people
because it is dressed
in overalls and
looks like work.

-THOMAS EDISON

WHERE THERE IS
NO STRUGGLE,
THERE IS
NO STRENGTH.

-OPRAH WINFREY

Grow Your Strength

Muscles that are not used will atrophy, while muscles that are exercised will grow and stay strong. The same is true throughout other aspects of our lives. Consider something moderately to extremely difficult that you're able to do today that you weren't able to do five or more years ago. What did it take to grow the strength you developed for that skill?

What personal characteristics did you draw on in order to see through the challenging times in order to reach that goal? How, if applicable, might those same characteristics help you today?

Write Your Mantra

You know what you want. You know why you want it. You know the sorts of things that may stand in your way—be it time, education, other people, or your own fears. How will you persevere when you stumble along the way? Write a mantra here to encourage yourself to keep on keeping on, even on hard days and despite obstacles expected and unexpected.

TENACITY

is when you follow your heart—
when the whole world is screaming
to get back into your head.

-SONIA CHOQUETTE

It's a slow process
REWRITING YOUR
OWN LIFE
in your head.

–EMMA HEALEY

♡

Hit Refresh

What, if anything, have you learned about yourself since beginning this journal? What would you like to better understand? How have your insights challenged old notions about yourself or your life? How might you rewrite your story now in a more positive, empowering, or honest way?

♡
Lose Yourself in an Upward Spiral

You've known the ease with which a downward spiral can take over your mind, and you may feel awkward in attempting its opposite, but give it a try. When in a positive headspace, visit this page and record:

What is great in your life?

What are you excited about?

What about it feels good?

What do you know you can do next?

If you can, give yourself some insight or inspiration—some fuel for your tomorrow self:

CONCENTRATION

IS A FINE

ANTIDOTE TO ANXIETY.

-JACK NICKLAUS

I've been searching for ways to heal myself, and I've found that

KINDNESS

is the best way.

-LADY GAGA

Be a Friend to Yourself

What is the meanest thing you tell yourself? It's time to confront that here. Bring forward a better side of yourself, and counter those negative statements with kindness, compassion, and healing.

Rise and Shine

Create a new habit for yourself by starting the day with a positive thought—something that leaves you feeling powerful, full of hope and promise. Jot down as many of these contemplations as you can below:

If you realized
how powerful
your thoughts are,
you would
never think a
negative thought.

-PEACE PILGRIM

If we are paying
attention to our lives,

we'll recognize those

DEFINING MOMENTS...

and opportunities that
—if jumped on—would get our
careers and personal lives
to a whole new level of

WOW.

-ROBIN SHARMA

Keep Watch on Your Life

It's easy to fall into a routine of reacting to life instead of acting assertively in pursuit of our own happiness. Ask yourself: What opportunity would you love to find for yourself in the future? Imagine an instinctive argument against pursuing that opportunity and counter it here with a combination of logic and a glass-half-full mentality:

Seed Your Success

Consider how every goal met begins with a single thought that we hold to and then nurture. What seeds from the past make up your present-day harvest? What seeds from the present could evolve into your future harvest?

What does that harvest need to grow and thrive?

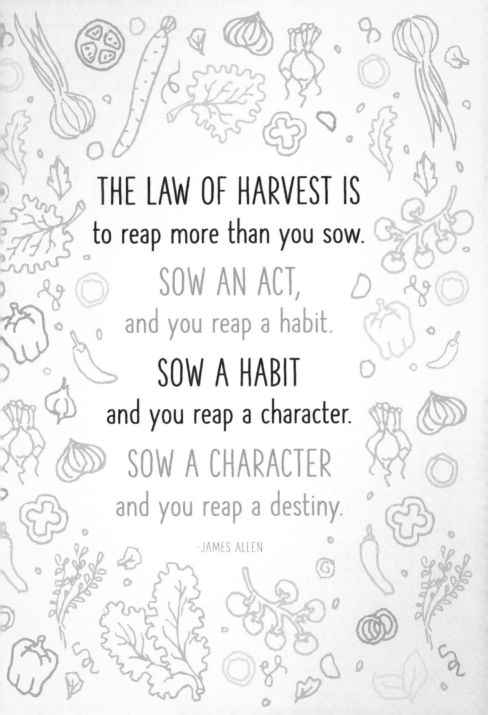

THE LAW OF HARVEST IS
to reap more than you sow.

SOW AN ACT,
and you reap a habit.

SOW A HABIT
and you reap a character.

SOW A CHARACTER
and you reap a destiny.

–JAMES ALLEN

Follow what you are
genuinely passionate about

and let that guide you
to your destination.

-DIANE SAWYER

Listen for the Heartbeat

Out of all the hopes and aspirations that cross your mind, which makes your heart sing the most? Which dreams shimmer with vibrancy in your imagination? Rank them, if you can.

Name the Dream of Dreams

What do you obsess about in the best way? Describe it and your love for this idea in glorious detail here:

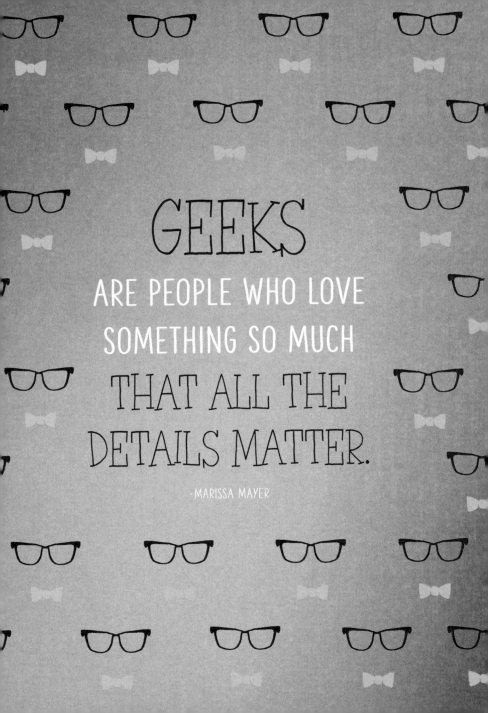

GEEKS

ARE PEOPLE WHO LOVE
SOMETHING SO MUCH
THAT ALL THE
DETAILS MATTER.

-MARISSA MAYER

You can find poetry
in your everyday life,
your memory, in what
people say on the bus,
in the news, or just
what's in your heart.

-CAROL ANN DUFFY

Find Your Fuel

What about the real world inspires you, and gives you hope for the future? Document a recent thought you had or a story about others—their beliefs, their actions, or their words—that encouraged you.

Honor the Human Experience

Sometimes we feel weak. We backslide. We say the wrong things, do the wrong things, and cause upset. Learn to forgive yourself and others for the very human ways we live our lives—imperfectly, even with good intentions in place.

Do you need to forgive yourself for something? Do you need to forgive someone else?

Fill in the following:

I used to think .... ,

but now I believe ....

...., and it's time to let it go.

I DON'T ALWAYS FEEL

FIERCE AND
FEARLESS,

BUT I DO FEEL LIKE
I'M A ROCK STAR
AT BEING HUMAN.

-TRACEE ELLIS ROSS

DWELL ON THE BEAUTY OF LIFE.

Watch the stars,
and see yourself
running with them.

-MARCUS AURELIUS

Seek Joy

Look around you and find five things, big or small, that bring you joy.
Write them here:

1.

2.

3.

4.

5.

Look within you with the same open spirit and list five things that you
love about yourself:

1.

2.

3.

4.

5.

Finish What You Start

There is a gift to finishing a thing, even when met with great resistance, even when it asks much of us. Even if there is no trophy or obvious change in your life, you move forward with the knowledge that you are strong and able to do hard things. What initiative have you abandoned? Write out what has dampened your drive for this goal and call out any doubts, fears, and irrational beliefs that got in the way. Remind yourself here why that goal meant something to you in the first place. How can you reconnect with it?

WHAT YOU GET
by achieving your goals
is not as important as
WHAT YOU BECOME
by achieving your goals.

-ZIG ZIGLAR

Live in each season
as it passes:

BREATHE THE AIR,

DRINK THE DRINK,

TASTE THE FRUIT.

-HENRY DAVID THOREAU

Focus on the Fruit

What nourishes hope in this season of your life? What are you grateful for, no matter what happens, no matter your mood? Take a few minutes to assess all of the "fruit" in your life, the small wonders that feed your spirit and renew your strength.

Honor Your Broken Parts

There is a practice called *kintsugi*, which involves repairing damaged pottery and highlighting the breaks with a golden lacquer, creating beautiful works of art.

What strengths are you proud to have earned through life experiences? What part of you, if any, feels broken or unhealed? How can you gild that break in gold, so that you can move forward despite loss?

The world breaks

EVERYONE,

and afterward,
some are strong
at the broken places.

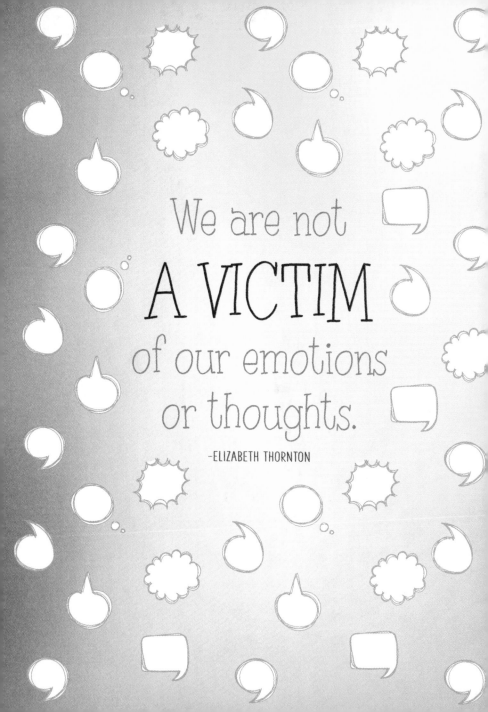

Make Action from Self-Knowledge

Throughout the course of this journal, you've excavated and examined your triggers to better understand what fuels them. How can you avoid or better manage those triggers? How does your knowledge of what makes you tick help you master your mood and claim more joy?

Build a Fire to Sustain You

Even with your best efforts, you'll occasionally find yourself in a dark headspace that is hard to shake. Learning how to find your inner light in those times is crucial. Keep fighting your way through the darkness. The next time you are trapped in a negative cycle, ask the experience that is taking something from you to give you something in return.

For every negative thought, write a constructive or encouraging counterthought or a statement of hope. Try it now in the space below.

You may not be able to do this right away. That's all right. Continue to try to develop this skill.

PEOPLE ARE LIKE
STAINED-GLASS WINDOWS...
Their true beauty
is revealed only
if there is a light
from within.

–ELISABETH KÜBLER-ROSS

THE TRUTH
WILL SET YOU FREE,
BUT FIRST IT WILL
PISS YOU OFF.

-GLORIA STEINEM

♡
Face Your Dragons

"Head work" isn't your enemy. Denial is. Consider all you've exposed about yourself—your fears, your beliefs, your strengths. See your spirals made of words, actions, and thoughts and recall they can often be countered with other words, actions, and thoughts. Look your paper dragons in the face, and then watch them fade. Give "head work" space in your life, and it in turn can help to illuminate who you are, which can power you through many of life's challenges.

Write yourself a prescription below. When, how, and for how long will you engage in "head work" moving forward?

♡
Take the Long View

Sometimes your best fuel can be borrowed from your future. Spend a few minutes detailing what your best future looks like.

How does your triumph look from the outside and feel on the inside?

What one word encapsulates your experience?

How will you share your story with others?

With whom will you share your joy?

The road to recovery
will not always be easy,
BUT I WILL TAKE IT
ONE DAY AT A TIME,
focusing on the moments
I'VE DREAMED ABOUT
FOR SO LONG.

-AMANDA LINDHOUT

FOREVER

IS COMPOSED OF

nows.

-EMILY DICKINSON

Craft Your Legacy

How do you want to be remembered? What good can you put into the world? What dreams are you determined to chase? What will matter most to you at the end of this journey?

♡

Hold Your Truths

You will have moments throughout your life when you know that something is true—about yourself, about others, about life in general. There may not be physical evidence, but you know it just the same, and those fundamental beliefs can create a power all their own. What are some things that you know in your heart to be true?

The best and most
beautiful things in the world
CANNOT BE SEEN OR
EVEN TOUCHED–THEY MUST
be felt with the heart.

–HELEN KELLER

THE PAGES ARE STILL BLANK,
but there is a miraculous
feeling of the words being there,
WRITTEN IN INVISIBLE INK
AND CLAMORING TO
BECOME VISIBLE.

-VLADIMIR NABOKOV